The Carpenter and The Unbuilder

The Carpenter and The Unbuilder

Stories for the Spiritual Quest

DAVID M. GRIEBNER

UPPER ROOM BOOKS

NASHVILLE

THE CARPENTER AND THE UNBUILDER: STORIES FOR THE SPIRITUAL QUEST
Copyright © 1996 by David M. Griebner
All rights reserved.

Scripture quotations not otherwise identified are from the New Revised
Standard Version of the Bible, copyright 1989 by the Division of Christian
Education of the National Council of the Churches of Christ in the USA
and are used by permission.

Illustrator: Paul Ritscher is one of the foremost wood-engravers practicing
in America today. His attention to fine detail is reminiscent of the master
engravers of a century ago. Self-taught from old illustrated books and
magazines, Mr. Ritscher's work shows a respect for the past fused with the
clarity of modern design. Used in a wide variety of graphic projects from
books, magazines, posters, and art prints, his work has won numerous
national and regional design awards. His prints are to be found in many
public and private collections, both in the United States and abroad.

Cover and interior design: Jim McAnally, Hand Jive Creative
Interior page layout: Nancy Cole
First Printing: June 1996 (7)

Library of Congress Cataloging-in-Publication Data

Griebner, David M., 1953–
    The carpenter and the unbuilder, stories for the spiritual quest / David
M. Griebner.
        p.   cm.
    ISBN: 0-8358-0778-9
    1. Religious fiction, American. 2. Fables, American. I. Title.
PS3557.R4878C37   1996
813' .54—dc20   96-4552
                                                       CIP

Printed in the United States of America

To the memory of

My father, Jack K. Griebner
My grandparents Clarence and Ruth Griebner
My grandfather Rev. Howard Burden,
who gave me a large measure of my faith, and
my grandmother Sylvia Burden, who was a storyteller

Also to

My mother Cathy Burden Griebner Tallady,
who has been a writer for as long as I can remember
My long-time spiritual friend Helen Collins,
who has helped many of these stories to come into the world

Most of all to

My wife, Sande, and my daughters Claire, Hannah, and Jordan

Contents

Foreword

Storytelling and Story Reading as Spiritual Disciplines

STORIES ARE AS OLD AS HUMAN LANGUAGE, and religious communities have long employed narratives to keep their teachings and traditions alive. First there are those stories that communicate particular values and reinforce particular behaviors within those communities. Recently there has been a resurgence of this type of story, championed by such volumes as *The Book of Virtues* and *A Call to Character*. A second type of story, the parables of Jesus for example, offers us a new and fresh perspective on the world and our own community's values and behaviors. Numerous scholarly and popular studies written over the past twenty years describe reversal of our expectations as a function of such parables. A third type of narrative explores that shadowy middle ground between mystery and meaning. In Islam the Sufis and in the Jewish tradition Hasidim are noted for such stories. A recent Christian practitioner of narrative as a spiritual discipline was the late Anthony DeMello. David Griebner's storytelling falls into this third category.

Many of you may have first encountered Griebner's brief parables in *Weavings: A Journal of the Christian Spiritual Life*. With brevity and directness of language, Griebner leads us through the familiar landscape of our hearts toward surprising epiphanies. Long before the Internet, there was the "Innernet" of images and metaphors that spoke of the deepest longings of humans everywhere. In *The Carpenter and the Unbuilder: Stories for the Spiritual Quest*, Griebner has logged onto this ancient worldwide web whose fragile threads connect the human depths of persons of vastly different ages and cultures. His stories are both deeply personal expressions of a profound relationship with God and universal avenues beyond everyday life and toward the realm of the holy that is too unruly to be tamed by mere language.

Griebner holds mystery and meaning in tension in his stories and allows the ambiguity of each narrative situation to carry the reader along to a deeper relationship with the God who will not remain captive to philosophical or theological categories. We religious folk attempt to contain and control the divine whimsy. In a sense, these stories free God from such a tidy filing-system approach. If there are more carpenters than unbuilders among us, it is because we are terrified that we will be swept away by the intensity of the relationship that the Holy One desires with us.

If the creation of such stories as the ones you will find in this slim volume is a spiritual discipline, then the reading and contemplation of them is as well. This is not the sort of book that you will want to devour in one sitting. Rather, I suggest that you read the stories one at a time, allowing each one to sink into your consciousness and begin to reshape your own relationship with God. If you allow a little time to cleanse your palate after each helping, you will derive the deepest delight as well as the most nourishment from such rich spiritual food.

— Michael E. Williams
Holy Innocents, 1995

Preface

THE STORIES IN THIS BOOK are very personal. First and foremost, they are the intimate expression of my evolving faith, self-awareness, and understanding of God. They are the product of the life, language, and imagination God has given me, and their life is connected to mine. So to begin, I want to tell you something about the role these stories play in my life. My hope is that these stories may encourage your faith and play a similar role, finding a like place in your life.

First, these stories point me in the direction of my own heart and center in God. Sometime after "The Carpenter and the Unbuilder" was published in *Weavings*, an Episcopal priest invited my wife and me to join him and his wife for dinner. As we were talking about the story I remember saying something like, "I just don't know where that story came from." This priest I had just met responded firmly, "Yes, you do." We talked some more and then the subject changed.

I have thought repeatedly about that simple exchange over the years, especially as each new story has emerged. Every story I have written so far has felt as if it were both a part of me and a part of something else—both a slice of my life and a slice of something far larger and more expansive than myself. I'd like to believe that these stories come from the part of me that is more directly in touch with God, perhaps the part of me that is more open to the grace of God.

When I write a story it is almost as if a door somewhere inside opens up, and an image or a thought emerges that often flows almost effortlessly into a complete story. Furthermore, I know as I read the finished product that I have had far less to do with this process than I imagine.

Thus, these stories are about my own spiritual journey and God's plan and purpose in my life. They appear to be one way God is able to lead me forward into greater understanding and intimacy.

Second, these stories seem to have the capacity to lead me back to my heart and center when I have lost my way. One time I was leading a retreat with a friend, and we decided that "The Carpenter and the Unbuilder" would serve as the focus for one activity. As I read the story to the group, I had the distinct feeling that someone else had written it. I felt as if I were reading it for the first time, and someone else was addressing me through the story. I remember protesting silently inside, *This is your story! You wrote it! How can this be?* Then I found myself appreciating it all over again, appreciating the holy place it had come from inside me but aware as well that it had come from a holy place that was beyond me. I found the story ministering to me with a life of its own.

Third, these stories are the intimate symbols of my

obedience to God. They are connected to what I believe is a deeper response to the presence of God in my life, and this response is both healing and energizing. As I write each story I feel as if I am doing precisely what God wants me to do at this moment in my life, and this is not for my purposes but for God's purposes. These stories are an act of surrender to the will of God as I understand it. For me this is probably the most satisfying thing about them.

Recently when "Between the Nails" was published in *Weavings*, I received a note from a woman I had come to know when I led a prayer retreat for her church. She told me how delighted she was to read the story in *Weavings*. She said that after reading it, she put it down and let wave after wave of awareness wash over her. When I read her note I thought to myself, *That's it. That's what happens to me. That's what I hope will happen in others.*

I pray that these stories will point you in the direction of your heart and center in God. I pray that they will lead you back to your heart and center when you have lost your way. And I dare to hope that they may play some small role in helping you discover and embrace the will of God for your life.

The stories in this book are very personal. They are the product of the life, language, and imagination God has given me, and their life is connected to mine. However, and more importantly, *I believe that my life is connected to these stories.* They are a living testimony to me that God is real, trustworthy, and good; that faith, hope, and love are possible. As such they are a sign of the new life God desires to give to me and to all.

My sincere hope is that in some small way the stories in this little book may serve God's purposes in your life and thus lead you to take a step or two toward your own dinner with the Holy One whose invitation to us is as personal as it is eternal.

The Carpenter and the Unbuilder:
The Invitation

Once upon a time there was a man living in a certain kingdom who received an invitation from his king to come to dinner. *Something* inside him was excited as never before by the invitation. *Something* was afraid as well. Would he have the right clothes to wear? Would his manners be good enough for his lord's table? What would they talk about when they were not eating? Above all, the man was frightened by the long journey to the king's castle.

So what did the man do? Well, he spent one month deciding what to wear and buying the clothes he did not already have. He spent two months learning the rules of etiquette and practicing them as he ate. He spent three months reading up on all the latest issues faced by the kingdom so he would have something to say.

Finally he faced the journey itself. By trade the man was a carpenter. He built small houses and extra outhouses and garages better than anyone else. After he had packed the clothing and food he thought he would need for the journey, he had room for only a little more. So he decided to pack a few tools, enough to permit him to build adequate overnight shelter on the journey. Then he started out.

The first day he traveled through the morning and early afternoon, stopping only to eat some lunch. Then he set about constructing a rough shelter to spend the night in. After a few hours labor he had a small, safe, dry place to sleep. The next morning as he was about to start out again, he looked at the shelter he had built. He began to notice places where it could be improved. So instead of resuming the journey right away, he began to make improvements on his little dwelling. Well, one thing led to another, garage to kitchen to indoor plumbing, and so on. Soon, he had pretty much forgotten about the invitation and the journey.

Meanwhile the king was beginning to wonder about the man. And so, as kings are able to do, he arranged for another person who was also traveling to the dinner to stop by and see how the man was coming along.

When the king's friend found him, the carpenter was living in his second house. He had sold the first one to someone, remembered the invitation, and moved on for a day or so. However, he had soon settled in and built an even bigger and better house on the profits he had made from the sale of his first one. The carpenter was only too happy to invite the visitor in for lunch; but while he was content to accept the offer of food, the visitor said he preferred to eat out in the yard under a tree.

"Is there a reason you don't want to come inside?" asked the carpenter, immediately wondering if his house wasn't quite right in some way.

"Why yes," replied the visitor. "You see, I am on a journey to have dinner with the king of our land. It is important for me to stay on the journey. Perhaps after lunch you would like to come with me?"

"What you say sounds familiar to me," said the carpenter. "I think I too received an invitation to have dinner with the king, but I have been a little bit uncertain of the way."

"I know," responded the stranger. "I was once uncertain as well. As a matter of fact, once I was a carpenter just like you. I too wanted to build safe places along the way to stay in. One day, another person on the journey helped me learn how to unbuild instead of to build. He helped me leave the house I was living in and trust the journey itself. I was worried about following the right path. He told me that there were a number of paths that would lead to the dinner. The king had set it up that way, and the king had also set up warnings along the wrong paths. The important thing was simply to put one foot in front of the other with love and trust. I was also worried about what I had left behind. To this he said that the king had seen to it that everything worth saving would be at the castle waiting for me."

"What you say is certainly of comfort. It helps to know that you have been just like me," said the carpenter.

"Well then, why don't we let go of this house and get on with the journey?"

"I don't know. Maybe. Can I sleep on it?"

"I suppose."

"May I fix a bed for you?"

"No," countered the visitor. "I will just stay out here under the tree. It is easier to notice the wonderful things the king has put along the way when you aren't looking out from inside something you have put up to protect yourself."

The unbuilder waited outside all night. The next morning the carpenter indeed had decided to resume the journey. Together they prepared to set out.

"Well," asked the carpenter. "Which way shall we go?"

"Which way seems right to you?" replied the unbuilder.

"I'm not sure."

"I'll tell you what. Let's just sit here a few minutes and think hard about the king. Remember the stories you have been told about him. Remember how much you love him. Remember how much he loves you. When you have remembered as clearly as you think you can, consider the paths that lie before you and see which one seems to satisfy your longing for, and remembrance of, the king. Let your desire to be with the king become more powerful in you than your uncertainty and fear about choosing the right or wrong path."

Silently they sat through the morning in the carpenter's front yard. Slowly it began to seem as though they were already on the journey. As that feeling grew and grew, it suddenly didn't seem like any decision needed to be made; it just happened. With a deep sense of freedom they were off.

Many of the days went just like that, new steps out of silent beginnings and pure desires. They simply waited until the sense of journeying wrapped itself around even their waiting, and then they were off without worrying whether they were on the "right" path or not. In the stillness of their hearts they made room for the path and the path seemed to come to them.

Of course the carpenter still felt the need to build a home from time to time. The unbuilder made sure he understood what he was doing and then let him do it if he really wanted to. While the carpenter labored, the unbuilder, his guide and friend, would continue the silent waiting in the yard under a tree, and soon they would unbuild yet another house and begin the journey again.

In the meantime the king kept the food warm, which he was very good at doing.

Shadowbound

Once upon a time there was a man who lived in the middle of a desert. Well, that was not quite true. It would be better to say that he was a prisoner of the desert. You see, somehow and sometime in the past our friend had acquired the habit of following his shadow, and only his shadow. It was a relentless and unbending compass that he obeyed completely and followed without question. Every morning when the sun came up, he began walking in the direction his shadow pointed. As the sun traced its slow crescent across the sky, he followed the subtle bending of his shadow. By the end of the day he had traced a rough oval and was nearly back to where he had started in the morning. While his course varied a little with the seasons of the year and the speed with which he walked, it wasn't much; and it was never enough to allow him to leave the desert.

This had been going on for as long as he could remember. It was familiar and comfortable, the only way he knew. Yet he also had to admit that it often left him feeling trapped and alone. Sometimes he wondered what it would be like to face the sun instead of always turning his back to it and walking the other way. And he longed to see if there might not be more to the world than the desert, but he never seemed to have enough resolve to do anything different.

Then one morning while it was still dark, as he was preparing to set out again, he heard a sound. It was a voice. At least it was more like a voice than anything else. It commanded, "Stop it." That's all, just "Stop it."

Stop it? He didn't know how he knew, but he knew

without a doubt that what was meant by this was his following his shadow. *Stop it.* Could it be that simple? What a lovely thought. Then again it was a fearful thought as well. Certainly there was joy and hope in what the Voice suggested, but there was also uncertainty, even dread, because following his shadow was the only way he knew to get around—such as it was!

About this time the sun came up and with it the powerful tug of his growing shadow. He tried to resist it but could not. Still all that day as he obediently followed his shadow, the memory of the Voice and the experience of the morning stayed with him. It stayed with him through the night too. And while he made no significant changes over the next few days, it was enough just to have some hope.

Then one morning, only a moment before the dawn, he suddenly turned his back to the dark, western horizon and faced the glow in the east. It was done almost before he realized what he was doing. The freedom to do it happened in a moment. And he recognized in his new freedom the presence again of the Voice, which lovingly offered him what he could not offer himself.

The rising sun in front of him was brighter and more wonderful than he imagined anything could ever be. As the sun cut across the sky that day, it was all he could do to stand there and face the light, turning slowly now to keep his shadow in back of him! As the day passed, his shadow became less and less intimidating and his new freedom more and more familiar, even if it were simply to stand still.

The next morning, the Voice came again. As before he could not fully describe what happened—only that the Voice brought another gift. This time the gift was a sense of direction.

Slowly he took a small step forward, fixed his gaze on some distant mountains, and set out. He wasn't sure where he was going, but at least he wasn't still going around in circles. And he certainly didn't feel alone anymore.

The Finder

The Finder stood there as he had many times before. In his hands he held familiar things: a pen, a wallet, a pair of eyeglasses, a sock, and a shoe.

"I believe these are yours," he said.

"Yes, I believe they are," murmured a man as he looked at what the Finder offered him. He was sitting up in bed. It was his room, and it was just before dawn. The Finder always came just before dawn.

"Shall I leave them then?" asked the Finder.

"Yes, if you please. Just put them on the dresser."

"As you wish," replied the Finder. He set the items down and then he was gone.

You see, the man in the bed was always losing something. One day it was a pen, his keys, his checkbook, and his glasses. The next day it was a book, a ring, his belt, and a sock. If an item weren't attached permanently, the chances were that he had lost it one time or another. If it weren't for the Finder, he probably wouldn't have had much of anything left at all. For before each dawn, the Finder would arrive in his room. He always carried everything the man had misplaced or lost throughout the day. Moreover, the conversation was always the same.

"I believe these are yours."

"Yes, I believe they are."

"Shall I leave them then?"

"Yes, if you please. Just put them on the dresser."

"As you wish," the Finder would reply. And then he would go.

One day the man lost a great deal. He left little bits and pieces of himself and his life all over town, more than at any other time. He even forgot where he lived and was glad when someone recognized him and offered to take him home. He had no idea how the Finder could gather it all up. But then he was there as always, just before dawn. His arms were full of things, including some items the man didn't immediately recognize as his. The Finder was as gentle as ever.

"I believe these are yours."

"Yes, I believe they are."

"Shall I leave them then?"

There was a pause before the man in the bed said, "No, I think not. You keep them."

"I'll save them for you then," responded the Finder.

"As you wish," said the man.

From that morning on that was how it went every day just before dawn, until everything he had was safely in the hands of the Finder. And then, he never lost himself again.

Between the Nails

$\mathcal{H}$e could hardly remember a day when there wasn't at least some pain, and this should come as no surprise. For you see, this man and all his people lived on a bed of nails. As you might guess, it was a rather prickly existence. However, as most people do, they had all gotten used to the particular limitations of their world. They accepted a certain amount of pain and discomfort as normal, and they had developed clothing and footwear that insulated them from most of the effect of the nails— although some were better at ignoring their pain than others.

Now for a long time the man had endured things as

they were, but then something in him began to grow restless. He became convinced that life had to be more than just managed discomfort. One day he decided there had to be a change. If not, he was going to take all his clothes off, jump up into the air and end it all. As he pondered what to do, he thought he heard something.

"Get small."

"What?" he asked. The word was out of his mouth before he had time to remember he was alone.

"Get small." There it was again. A Voice. He was sure of it. Sort of. Someone was talking to him. And since he was out of other options at the moment, he decided to talk back.

"Who are you?"

"Get small."

"What do you want?"

"Get small."

Obviously he wasn't asking the right question. He decided to address the advice directly.

"What do you mean, 'Get small?'"

"Get small." Apparently this was all he was going to get, and his next response came mostly out of a sense of frustration.

"I can't get small!" he yelled.

"I can make you small," whispered the Voice.

Well, there it was then. If he accepted that the Voice was real, the only thing left to do was to trust what the Voice had to say.

"All right," he declared. "Make me small."

The first thing he noticed was that his clothes got big. Then the nails got big. Then the space between the nails got big, and he found himself between the nails. Then the space between the nails got so big there was more space than nails. Then there was so much space it seemed as if there were no nails at all. Then he was surrounded by people. They brought him light, airy clothes to wear and wonderful food that was as rich as the ground was smooth. It was strange feeling, but it seemed like he had finally come home.

Once a week he and all the people between the nails gathered together to sing. They lifted their voices to the heavens and sang with all their heart the two words the Voice had taught them all. "Get small," they sang.

And day by day the Lord added to their number those who were being saved.

Blindsided

*T*hey had been sitting there facing each other for longer than either of them could remember. In fact, it was a staring contest. The first one to blink lost everything. However the funny thing was that they had been at it for so long they were both completely blind! So each one sat there in his chair unblinking, unable to tell if he had finally won. All either one knew for sure was that he hadn't lost yet. Suddenly both were aware of a Third Person in the room with them. They both heard her at the same time.

"Hey, you!" they cried in unison.

"Yes," came the reply from the stranger. "What can I do for you?"

Without so much as a moment's hesitation they both said, "Tell me, has he blinked yet?"

"I can't tell," offered the Third Person. "The lights have been out in this room for quite some time." Then she continued, "But I know a place where a light shines, which is brighter than the darkness in this room. It is brighter than the darkness between you and brighter than the darkness in you. I will take you there if you want me to."

The two contestants were silent for a long time. Finally, one of them spoke.

"I want to go," he announced. He stood up and reached out for the hand he knew surely must be there in the darkness, extended toward him. Together he and the Third Person waited a long time for his opponent to make a decision. When there was no response, they left.

Sometime later the one left sitting there staring at a now empty chair said, "Good try, but you can't fool me."

I imagine he is still there, staring alone into the darkness; and all he knows for sure is that he hasn't lost—yet.

The Visit of the Wader

Once there was a river and in a place nearby— a place that everyone agreed was a safe distance away from the river—there was a village. As far as the people of the village knew, this river was the only source of fresh water anyone had ever found. For this they were grateful, and for this they revered the river as a source of life.

However, they were all aware that the river could be unpredictable and dangerous as well. There was a story, which everyone in the village knew, about a time long ago when the river overflowed its banks and washed away a former village, killing nearly everyone. So while they loved the river, they also feared it. To reconcile their need for the water and their fear of the river, the villagers designated one person each day to go down to the river and gather enough water for the entire village. All able-bodied villagers were expected to take their turn. With this arrangement the whole village enjoyed the benefits of the water without putting them all at undue risk.

One day when the designated person went down to the river to begin the first of several trips to gather enough water for the community's needs, she was shocked to find someone standing in the middle of the river. This was unthinkable! Didn't he know how dangerous it was to do what he was doing! She opened her mouth to warn the person. But before she could speak, he gestured to her and gently invited her to come wading with him. This was more than she could bear, and she raced back to the village. Breathlessly she told everyone her story. They were all curious, but none of them wanted to make an unscheduled trip to the river to see if it were true. They decided that the prudent thing to do was to conserve what water they had and wait until tomorrow. Perhaps then the stranger would be gone.

However the next day, he was still there. And he invited the person sent to gather that day's water to join him as well. Although the villager declined, he was able to compose himself enough to bring back the water his people needed.

Days passed and "The Wader," as they chose to call him, stayed in the middle of the river. He greeted each one who came to gather water and invited him or her to come wading. But while the people of the village became better at gathering what they needed without undue panic, none of them accepted the invitation.

The Wader stayed in the river, offering his gentle invitation, until everyone in the village had been to gather water. Then he was gone. But the people of the village remembered his visit. They even wrote a story about it, and this new story began to challenge their beliefs about the river. So it happened that over time, more and more of the villagers came back from gathering water at the river with their pants rolled up and river bottom mud between their toes.

And year by year the villagers moved their homes closer and closer to the river.

The Journal with the
Words Already in It

It was sometime in her twenties, she remembered, that she had begun writing her thoughts down in a journal. When she began, it was as if someone had taken her lid off and given her a place to pour out who she was and what she hoped for. The empty pages of her journal also provided a safe place to express her anger.

At first she filled up just one page a day, but gradually her writing increased. Soon she was buying a new journal once a month and sometimes even more often. Filling it up continued to be a source of joy and relief to her, but slowly the process of recording her thoughts became less and less satisfying. Some days she felt like a dog or a cat chasing its tail; writing seemed to release some pent up pressure, but she wasn't getting anywhere.

One day, having filled up a large journal in less than a month, she went down to the store to buy a new one. She decided that while she was there she would buy two and save another trip. The same clerk as always was behind the counter.

"Buying another journal I see," he commented.

"Yes."

"And is the other one for a friend?" he wondered aloud.

"No, they're both for me," she said. "I seem to be filling them up faster and faster."

"Have you ever thought of trying a different journal?" he continued.

"You mean a larger one?" she responded.

"No, not exactly," he replied. "One with some words already in it."

"You mean like poetry or a verse from the Bible?"

"Not exactly," he said. "Here, try this one for a few days. My gift to you."

She accepted his gift, put one journal back, and paid for the remaining one. When she got home she began with her regular book. She filled it up faster than ever and was left emptier than ever. As she put the last word on the last page, she remembered the clerk's gift. The next day she picked up this journal. Glancing through it she saw that words *were* already in it—but not very many. Indeed they only covered the first six pages. There was a single thought on each page. The first day she read this: "Walk down the short hallway." The second day she read, "Pray My prayers." The third day: "Think My thoughts." The fourth day: "Live My life with Me now." So it went through all six days until something like a poem emerged. Altogether it read like this:

Walk down the short hallway.
Pray My prayers.
Think My thoughts.

Live My life with Me now.
And when it is time to walk down the long hallway,
Live your life with Me forever.

For six days she read just one line each day and then wrote her own thoughts beneath it. Each day she noticed that she wrote a little bit less than the day before. On the seventh day she looked over all the words that preceded hers in the book:

Walk down the short hallway.
Pray My prayers.
Think My thoughts.
Live My life with Me now.
And when it is time to walk down the long hallway,
Live your life with Me forever.

Now the page in front of her was blank. She thought for a moment—maybe longer. Then she put down her pen, closed the journal, and walked down the short hallway to embrace the peace she had sought for so long.

God's Gold

*O*nce there was an ordinary young man. As a matter of fact, the only extraordinary thing about this young man was his great-aunt. She was truly great in more ways than you or I could imagine. Since this young man had grown up and moved away from home, he hadn't spent much time with his great-aunt. Actually he hadn't seen her in years.

We can understand then why he wasn't terribly upset when she died. However, he became more interested when he learned that his aunt had remembered him in her will.

He didn't hope for much money because she had always been an humble woman, far more generous than she was rich. Then again, one never knew, and it just might be that she had wealth no one imagined.

His fantasies had become quite elaborate by the time he arrived at the lawyer's and were dashed only slightly when he was given what his great-aunt had left him: a key and a note. The note said the key was to a room in her apartment. It said further that if he wanted, he could go to the apartment and take what was in the room. *What could it be?*

He went to the apartment, found the room, turned the key in the lock, and opened the door. Inside was a single table. On the table sat a pure white pitcher. Next to the pitcher was another note. Other than these three items, the room was empty. He read the note:

In this pitcher is the gold of God.
You may empty it once a day,

and it will always be full the next.
But take care,
for only one vessel
will hold this gold long enough
for it to be of any use to you.

With growing disappointment and much disbelief
and skepticism, he looked inside the pitcher. Sure enough
something gold-looking was in it. But the gold of God?
Come on! Then again, what could it mean? Was it some
sort of joke? Was it a puzzle that would lead him to
some real gold if he figured it out? He looked around for
something to pour the pitcher's contents into, but there was
nothing else in the room. Well, she said he could have what
was in the room if he wanted. He didn't want the table, so
he took the pitcher and the note home with him.

Once inside his own house, he got a glass. He tipped
the pitcher forward; a stream of something gold poured out
and filled up the glass. Then suddenly—almost before the

pitcher was empty—it began to disappear, as if the glass had a hole in the bottom. Soon there was nothing left in the glass and nothing left in the pitcher. He went back and reread the note.

In this pitcher is the gold of God.
You may empty it once a day,
and it will always be full the next.
But take care,
for only one vessel
will hold this gold long enough
for it to be of any use to you.

It must mean what it says, he thought. He waited until the next day. Sure enough the pitcher was full again. This time he carefully considered what sort of vessel might hold this "gold." He tried a pan from his kitchen. *Metal to hold metal*, he thought, but again the "gold" ebbed away. Over the next few weeks he tried one container after another. He tried containers made of different materials and in different shapes. He even sneaked into the church one day and poured it into the chalice. Unfortunately the result was always the same, and then he had to wait another day to try again.

As time went on, he became obsessed with the pitcher and its contents. At the same time, he wondered what had come over him. After all, it only looked like gold. It never stayed around long enough for anyone to prove it was one thing or another. But try as he might, he could not go a day without pouring it into something new or different.

One day as he was pouring the contents down the slender neck of an exotic Chinese vase, he spilled some on his hand. It startled him so much he almost dropped the pitcher. He had never considered what might happen if he got some of the stuff on himself! His first thought was to wipe it off as quickly as possible, and he nearly fell while lunging for the towel by the sink. Strangely enough, when he went to wipe it off he discovered that the gold had stayed on his hand no longer than it ever stayed anywhere else, and now it too was gone. All that was left was a slight warmth, but even that was fading away now. He stared at his hand for a long time, rubbing the spot where the "gold" had landed. Then he got out the note from the room and read it one more time.

In this pitcher is the gold of God.
You may empty it once a day,
and it will always be full the next.
But take care,
for only one vessel
will hold this gold long enough
for it to be of any use to you.

That evening he pondered the note's message once again. Sometime in the middle of the night he knew what he was going to do. It should have terrified him, but it didn't. As a matter of fact, he wondered why he hadn't thought of it sooner.

The next morning he took the pitcher, raised it to his mouth, pressed his lips to its softly turned edge, tilted his head back, and drank.

When he died many years later some of his old friends remarked how his life had changed shortly after his great-aunt had died. Others could only say that for them he had shone like the sun and had lifted their faith on more than one occasion. Still others called him a saint. His great-niece, who hadn't seen him in years, simply wondered about the meaning of the note and key he left her in his short will.

The Carpenter and the Unbuilder:
Even Our Brokenness

The more the carpenter and the unbuilder traveled together, the more the carpenter understood

what it meant to build a house. He understood something about his insecurity, his fearfulness, and how hard it was to trust when you couldn't quite see your destination. And the more he became aware of these weaknesses, the more often he felt guilty and angry with himself. He felt bad when he was building a house; and even when he moved on, the memory of the last house he had built—or maybe even the house before that—continued to haunt him.

One day after he had decided to leave a particularly nice little place he had built, the unbuilder could see that the carpenter was very discouraged. As they were leaving the little house and the valley in which he had built it, the unbuilder stopped.

"Look back for a moment," the unbuilder said gently.

As the carpenter turned around, he saw his former home and, in the distance, a woman. She had just entered the valley from the other side. She looked very tired, and she was alone. In fact, she looked as if she could hardly take another step. However, when she saw his recently abandoned dwelling, she seemed to gain new strength. With quickening steps she moved to the house and knocked on the door. Receiving no answer, she went inside.

The carpenter looked at the unbuilder for an explanation. The unbuilder spoke carefully, "Once you have left your original home and accepted the invitation to dinner, every step on the journey links you to all who are on their way to dinner. Sometimes the home that you build out of your need and then let go of or leave behind, can help another traveler. Not everyone can do what you do. Not everyone will welcome someone like me. The king cares for his travelers in many ways. That woman was about to turn around and abandon the journey. Your former home will provide the shelter she needs until she is ready to resume her journey."

At that moment the carpenter felt as if a great weight, or sorrow, left him; he turned and walked over the crest of the hill, more eager than ever to be on his way.

My Salvation and Yours

Once there was a woman who made stained-glass windows for a living. Now I know what you are thinking, but she didn't make the kind of windows that had people in them or scenes from the Bible. Instead her delight was in the color of the glass. She had a special gift for putting colors together, so she worked mostly with large pieces of wonderfully colored glass, which she arranged beautifully. She was satisfied and so were her customers.

Then one night she had a dream that would change everything. In her dream it felt as if Someone spoke to her and, seemingly, placed an order: "Make me a window of my salvation and yours." When she woke up she remembered the dream for a few minutes, as we often do, and then she forgot it. However, the dream returned the next night, "Make me a window of my salvation and yours."

Soon she was having this dream every night. Thus, even though she didn't understand the request exactly, she decided to make a window for the sake of a good night's sleep. She wondered where to begin. She decided to do what she did best. She gathered some beautiful pieces of stained glass, arranged them in a way that seemed right to her, and leaded the whole thing together. She went to sleep that night expecting to be left alone. She was not. "Make me a window of my salvation and yours."

She walked toward her studio the next morning uncertain what to do now. *Should she make another window? Move to another town? See a psychiatrist?* Then her thoughts were interrupted by what she saw when she opened the door. Her beautiful window had somehow tipped over and shattered on the concrete floor. *How? Now what? Is this why the dream came back?* She sat there for a few moments looking at the fragments of her window. Then, despite her own resistance and uncertainty, she picked up a piece of the broken glass and another and another. Somehow she could see how these pieces went together even more beautifully now than they had when they were larger. She worked through the day and by evening she had a new window. While it was the same glass as before, now there were many more pieces and much more detail. In fact the window contained more pieces than she had ever worked with before. She was happy with her work, and she went to sleep exhausted. Surely this window was enough she thought, but she was wrong. The same Voice as before unsettled her sleep: "Make me a window of my salvation and yours."

Weary and angry she stayed away from her studio all the next morning. When she finally opened the door after lunch, a sight greeted her that she almost expected. Her latest window was in pieces on the floor—far more pieces than the last time! Fighting despair and the urge to run away, she cradled her head in her hands and peered out at the broken glass through the space between her fingers. After several painful and uncertain moments, she tenderly reached out with one hand and put two pieces of glass together . . . then another.

It took her longer than a day to make a window this time. There were so many pieces and so many ways to arrange them. Oddly enough, while she was working on this window her dreams were silent. This silence left her hopeful. Finally her latest window was done as well. The pieces of glass were so small it was almost like a mosaic. And it was beautiful. She hadn't imagined that she was capable of creating such beauty. Surely now her dreams would be silent, but it wasn't to be. The very night after she finished she heard again, "Make me a window of my salvation and yours."

So it went. She made window after window; every one was broken in its turn, each time into smaller and smaller pieces. Thus each subsequent window became more and more detailed, etched with subtler and subtler shades of color and beauty and wonder. In a way she became accustomed to the dream and to the breaking down and the building up.

Then one day she died. Her friends found her in her studio. Next to her was a pile of tiny slivers of glass. They left the pile undisturbed, closed the studio, and locked the door. But on the day of her funeral, a great wind broke through the window of the place, swept up that pile of fine glass and cast it into the sky where it ignited in the sun like a million rainbows. At her funeral some said they heard a voice say "Well done" just as the preacher finished the prayer.

It's All Right

One day a man came home after a long day at work.

I suppose you could say that it had been a pretty normal day. He had awakened that morning with the usual mixture of anticipation and dread, excitement and boredom, satisfaction and regret—and a host of other emotions and attitudes not so easily labeled. His life didn't leave him feeling entirely whole, but he couldn't find anything that needed immediate attention either. Somewhere along the way, he had come to accept his own ambivalence as the way things were meant to be.

He walked into his house, closed the door and locked it behind him. He didn't plan on going out again that

night. Almost immediately, he regretted locking himself
in. A light was on in the kitchen, and he heard a noise as
if someone were in there. Before he could react one way or
another or even say anything, the kitchen door opened and
he stood face to face with . . . himself! At least that's who
it looked like. Not only was it like looking in a mirror,
but the intruder was eating what he had planned to eat for
dinner and was wearing the clothes that should have been
upstairs in his closet!

The effect the two of them had on each other was pure
paralysis. They simply stared at each other, too surprised
to move. But while there was little movement going on
between them, lots of things were happening around them.
A key turned in the door and in walked another image of
himself. This one stopped half in and half out of the door
when he saw the two of them. Another one came down the
stairs dressed in his gym shorts, wearing his sneakers, and
toting his tennis racquet.

Over and over again it happened. One image after
another, differing only in slight variations of dress and

purpose, walked through the door or came up from the basement or walked down the stairs. When they saw one another, they all stood there full of disbelief, confusion, and—if he were any measure of the rest of them—immense fear.

Suddenly One was in the room who was not one of them. He moved slowly and deliberately from image to image. He approached each one, placed his hands over the ears, looked the image straight in the face, said something, and moved on. As he moved throughout the room and touched one after the other, it seemed that the house was becoming less and less crowded. Finally he came to the man we started with, cupped his hands over our friend's ears, looked him straight in the face, and spoke carefully and distinctly, "It's all right."

As the words blew across his face, the man suddenly found himself alone in the room. Despite the unusual events of the past few minutes, he felt a sense of wholeness and peace that was unlike anything he had ever felt before. And he couldn't wait to see what was going to happen next!

Fire Fall

A long time ago there were some people who were the first of their world to discover fire. Fortunately they seemed to know how important a discovery this was, and they treated the fire with supreme respect and reverence. Furthermore they were a generous people, and they were more than willing to give their fire away to anyone who wanted it. All they asked was that those to whom they gave it agreed to use it according to the rules. No one knew exactly where the rules had come from, but they seemed to have existed for at least as long as fire itself. The rules centered around a warning that was so frightening no one had ever dared try to prove it right or wrong. The warning was this: If any flame ever came into contact with the ground, it could set the earth itself on fire.

For this reason they were very careful to build every fire outside on a precisely arranged pile of stones that easily put the flames two, three, or even four feet off the ground. Only this arrangement could assure that nothing ever filtered down to the ground except a few cold ashes, and so they felt safe. The people had distilled these rules that governed their use of fire into four sacred sayings. They went like this, and they accompanied every gift of fire:

Let those who use fire beware,
Build it on stones, in the open air.
Lest fire touch and bring to birth,
Flames to consume the earth.

So these people made a kind of uneasy peace with this great gift. However, one day they heard some news that sparked an immediate feeling of horror. Apparently a small group of strangers was moving through the outlying villages. They were visiting the very people with whom the gift of fire had been shared. Furthermore, the strangers were teaching that the true place for fire was on the ground and in one's home; and contrary to all reason, they were teaching that there was nothing to fear. They even changed the four sacred sayings and replaced them with sayings of their own that went like this:

Let everyone embrace the fire!
Tear down every stony pyre.
Let fire fall and bring to birth,
Flames to transform the earth.

This was bad enough. But even worse were the stories that some people had acted on this dangerous teaching.

They were building their fire on the ground and some
may have even taken it inside their home. This information
was more than these people could bear. Their worst fears
seemed to be coming true. Terrorized, they stopped giving
away the fire they had; but they could not undo what had
been done. From then on the world was divided into two
kinds of people.

There were those who accepted the new sacred sayings.
They discovered that when they placed the fire on the
ground and took it inside their homes, the earth was not
set on fire at all. Instead their homes were warmer, the
great gift was easier to use, and it was a delight to share
it without fear.

Then there were those who held to the old ways. They
kept their fire to themselves and spent their lives looking
for the perfect stones to make the perfect piles to keep their
little fires safely away from their little plots of dirt.

The Toe in the Mirror

Once there was a rich man who entertained himself by collecting things. One day in an antique store, he was intrigued to discover what appeared to be a large, full-length mirror. He couldn't be sure because all he could see was the frame. A heavy canvas covered what was most likely a mirror. A faded piece of paper pinned to the canvas read "Do Not Remove." He called for the store owner.

"What is this and why is it covered?" he asked. He was used to getting his way.

"You won't believe me," came the reply.

"Tell me anyway," he demanded. Again, he was used to getting his way.

"Well," continued the clerk. "Under the canvas is a mirror. The story is that this mirror will only reflect the part of you that is alive in God. I keep it covered because it's bad for business. Too many people don't see what they expect to see."

"You let people look if they want to?"

"Not usually but some people insist. Mostly they are the ones who don't believe me. Once they take the canvas off and look, they tend to leave in a hurry without buying anything. As I said, it's bad for business."

"May I look."

"If you must."

The wealthy man thought for a moment. Then, reassured by the knowledge that his accountant kept his church pledge up to date, he peeled the canvas aside and stood full in front of the mirror.

"I don't see anything!" he shouted, wondering immediately if the light was bad.

"There's always been something before," responded the

owner, sympathetic from a certain amount of practice in such situations. "Look again."

He looked up and down the mirror. Sure enough something was there. Down in the corner near the bottom, like a lonely radish, was his big toe.

"My toe," he mumbled. "That's all there is."

"That's all for now," replied the clerk.

"You mean it can change?"

"So some say."

"Name your price for the mirror."

The store owner wasn't all that unhappy to see the mirror go.

The collector took the mirror home with him. Many times each day he stood in front of the mirror, but nothing ever changed. Only the big toe of his left foot was visible. He tried everything to alter this one annoying fact. He stood in front of the mirror in a $2000 hand-tailored suit. He stood there with all his bank and stock broker statements. Nothing. He stood there with his award from a service club for his help during their last fund raiser. He paraded in front of the mirror holding a certificate of dismissal from a well-known and highly respected psychotherapist. He went to church every week— sometimes twice!—and always saved the bulletin to show the mirror. Zip. Zero. No response—nothing but that single big toe.

At last he gave most of his money away. As he stood before the mirror, he thought he detected a small change in the image of his toe, which gave him some hope. A closer examination revealed that it was only that his toenail had grown and needed clipping.

Finally there was nothing left for him to pursue. He had no new ideas, nothing more to offer the mirror. Still he could not stop looking at it and thinking about it. In his helplessness he broke down in front of the mirror and cried. He wept for his weakness and his emptiness. He wept out of frustration, and he wept for reasons he couldn't begin to explain.

Then in the next moment, he let go. He let go of his need to be in control of everything. He let go of his need to figure out how the mirror worked. His heart opened not to how he desired to know the Mystery of the mirror but to how the Mystery of the mirror desired to be known. His eyes were so full of tears that he did not notice, dimly at first, and then with greater and greater definition, his other toes, foot, feet, legs, arms, torso, shoulders, neck, and head filling up the mirror.

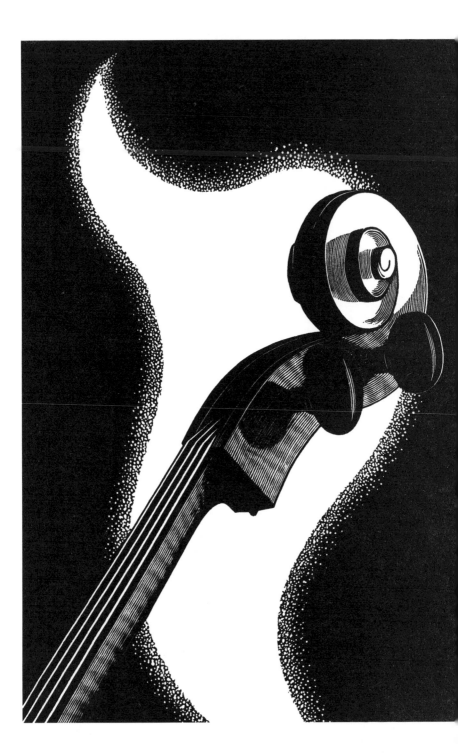

Sheer Desire

*O*ne day in a large city, in a large stone church that was right downtown and open most of the time, a man went in and sat down in one of the pews. This was not unusual. Many people came in during the day to sit for a while in the great holy space of the church. But this man stayed. He had been sitting there all day long when the minister decided she had better go talk to him. The man looked like anyone else who might wander in off the street to sit in the church for a few moments—with two minor exceptions. Next to him in the pew he had a butterfly net and a knapsack. The minister felt a momentary sense of restraint but spoke anyway.

"May I help you?" she inquired.

"Yes," replied the man. "I have come looking for something of God."

The minister's uneasiness shifted a little bit in the direction of interest. Not everyone would name this kind of hunger to her. However her joy passed quickly as the man continued.

"And when I find something of God I will snatch it up in my butterfly net and put it in my knapsack and pull the cord tight and have God always with me forever."

The minister didn't want to discourage the man, but she couldn't exactly leave his statement unchallenged either. She spoke in her best and most gentle theological voice.

"I don't think that you can just scoop God up into a butterfly net or into a knapsack," she offered, not even wanting to comment on the "forever" side of the man's desire.

"I know that," came the reply. "I didn't say I wanted to scoop *God* up in my butterfly net. I said I was looking for something *of* God that I could snatch up with my net and put in my knapsack and have God always with me forever."

The minister was torn between trying to explain to the man that there wasn't much difference between the two and the feeling that anything of God in the church that the man could put into his net would likely be stealing, when the matter was taken out of her hands. The man looked at his watch, picked up his net and knapsack, and left.

However the next day he was back, and he sat in the church the whole day again. The same thing happened for all the rest of the days that week and Sunday as well. Of course the man was the center of some animated conversation. Many people came up to him and introduced themselves. Some withdrew to a safe distance when the man explained the purpose of his butterfly net and knapsack, but others sincerely tried to listen and help. Yet nothing seemed to change the man's stated intent.

Over time he became a kind of fixture in the church. The people greeted him warmly, and they began to appreciate his presence and to see themselves as his caretakers. The man never changed much and never did much and never said much. Occasionally he joined in the services, often he just sat there. To everyone who ever asked him what he was about, he simply said, "I have come to find something of God. And when I do I will snatch it up in my butterfly net and put it in my knapsack and pull the cord tight and have God always with me forever."

So it went until one day as he was sitting there in the church the man was overcome by a great drowsiness. He fell asleep in the pew for just a few minutes. When he woke up, he immediately sensed that something was different. He quickly picked up his butterfly net. He was ready to pounce. However when he looked at the net he saw that while he was asleep someone had cut the bottom out of it. He checked his knapsack. The bottom of it was gone too.

Some others sitting nearby noticed the changes as well. They saw the man staring through the holes in the shorn net and the gutted knapsack. They were terrified for him.

Someone went to get the minister. Others gathered around ready to offer their support because, as far as they knew, the net and knapsack made up most, if not all, of this man's life. As the minister came running, she was thinking about how quickly they might be able to replace the man's ruined equipment. Silently they all gathered around. The minister was about to say something helpful and comforting when the man spoke first.

With a huge grin, he repeated two words over and over. "At last," he said. "At last."

Heart and Center

*O*nce upon a time there was a man who lived in the forest. He had lived in the forest his whole life, and he was not alone. Other people lived nearby in the forest and within a short distance were groups of even more people. Often they would get together and tell stories and poems. One of the poems they told was very old and it went like this:

> *In the center of the forest*
> *In the heart of the center*
> *Is the Keeper of the forest.*

Who sees to it

> *That the leaves come out in their season to*
> ~~cover the trees~~
> *And fall off in their season to cover the earth.*

Who sees to it

> *That the mushrooms appear in their season*
> *for food*
> *And the wild flowers appear in their season*
> *for beauty.*

In the heart of the forest
> *In the center of the heart*
> > *Is the Keeper of the forest.*

All his life he had heard stories of people who went off looking for the heart and center and Keeper of the forest. He had a great longing to know of their experience and if they ever found what they had set out to find. One day he decided it was time for him to see what, if any, truth there was to the poem. He said good-bye to his friends, packed some supplies, and set out. Since he didn't know which way to go, he simply picked a path at hand and followed it further than ever before.

Around noon he ran into another traveler on the path. "Can you tell me how to get to the center of the forest?" he asked.

"The center of the forest?" came the reply. "There is no such place. I've known people all my life who have left home and tried to find the center of the forest. None ever came back having found it." Then he added ominously, "Some never came back. So, don't waste your time. Just make the best life you can for yourself, by yourself, and be content with that." Then he was gone in a hurry to do something important.

The man walked on for a while. Soon he saw a woman sitting down next to the path. "Can you tell me how to get to the center of the forest?" he asked.

"I certainly can, but I don't know why you'd want to go there. I found it recently after a long search, and I was crushed by what I found. Nothing. There is nothing there. All my searching for nothing, . . . nothing, . . . nothing." She continued to mumble the same word softer and softer. Clearly he wouldn't get any useful directions from her, so he moved on.

By now he had pushed far into a part of the forest he had never seen before. In a clearing straight ahead, a well-dressed person stood under a sign that announced, "Maps to the center of the forest!" He couldn't believe his good fortune, and although the price of the map was rather steep and the smile of the seller a little too bright, he bought one anyway and started following it. It didn't take him long to follow all the directions and turns on the map. But where he ended up didn't appear to be any different than any other place he had been. A brief question to a passerby confirmed his suspicions.

"Is this the center of the forest?" he asked.

"You are the third person today to ask me that question," was the somewhat annoyed reply. "I've lived in this grove of trees my whole life, and I've never heard anyone call it the center of the forest before today. I can't imagine why so many people would want to know the answer to that question all of a sudden!"

Our friend thought about retracing his steps to the map seller, but he was pretty sure the little stand would be gone. So he walked on. After a while he sat down. He had a choice to make. He could give up his search and try to find his way back home, or he could go on looking for the center of the forest, which no one seemed to have any idea how to find. As he was thinking, a woman sat down next to him.

"You look lost," she commented tenderly.

"I don't know whether I'm lost or not. I've been looking for the center of the forest. So far I haven't been able to find it, and I haven't found anyone who can help me find it."

"Are you looking for a way to get *there* from *here?*"

"Why, yes, of course!" There was excitement in his voice.

"Then, I must tell you that there is no center of the forest such as you are looking for."

"How do you know?" he questioned defensively.

"Have you ever climbed a tree tall enough so that you could look out over the top of the forest?" she continued.

"Yes."

"What did you see?"

"All around me, as far as I could see, were the tops of trees. That's all."

"Precisely. What you saw from the top of that tree was the same thing you would see from the top of any tree anywhere in the forest. This forest goes on forever. From anywhere in the forest, it goes on forever in all directions. No matter where you are, the forest goes on forever in every direction. Do you understand?"

He wasn't sure if he did or not, but he replied anyway, "I guess so, but how is this important for me? I want to find the center of the forest and the heart of the center and the Keeper of the forest—not the edge of the forest."

She went on, "Suppose you are standing in a place where everything goes on forever in every direction.

Imagine that no matter where you are, everything goes on for the same distance in every direction, north, south, east and west. If you were in that place where would you be?"

"If everything went on forever in every direction, the same distance all around, I guess I'd be in a kind of a . . . center." He stopped and his new friend let him stop.

"I'd be in the center! And the center would be where I was. It would be wherever I was, kind of, sort of . . . " This thought was so new and different that it took a moment to sink in. He remembered the beginning and the end of the poem that called him to the journey.

> *In the center of the forest*
> *In the heart of the center*
> *Is the Keeper of the forest.*
> *In the heart of the forest*
> *In the center of the heart*
> *Is the Keeper of the forest.*

He looked around for the stranger, but she was gone. Then he smiled and began the long walk back to his friends. Or maybe not!

Your Own Voice

She found herself sitting in a large room. It was like a big auditorium with a stage down in front. She was aware of others in the room with her, but she didn't look around to count them all. She seemed to be there for some reason, but she wasn't quite sure what it was.

A door at the front of the room opened. A man walked in and stood there. They all looked at him. He appeared disoriented. He glanced up at them and then looked back at the door from which he had entered. He took a step forward and then immediately retreated. He looked around furtively as though someone should be there to tell him what to do.

Apparently he wasn't sure why he was there either. Then he changed: He straightened himself up, looked directly at them, and walked to the front of the stage.

Even though she had seen him for the first time only a moment before, it was as if everything about him was different—like he had grown up all of a sudden. Now he appeared to know exactly where he was, and strength and confidence replaced the confusion and uncertainty of the moment before. With a comforting self-assurance that commanded their attention he declared with joy,

We are going to sing.
We are going to sing with One Voice.
We are going to sing all together.
The same notes with One Voice.
We are going to sing beautifully with One Voice,
   all together.

He paused a moment, smiled, and then added, "And when you find the One Voice that is your Own Voice, it will be time for you to leave."

With that he began to sing. At first it was just one note. He held the pitch there for the group to find, waited until everyone got it just right, and then added another. The second note was a perfect complement to the first. Soon there were many notes. Each note was just the right one to follow the note before and lead into the one to come. Together they sang simple, joyful songs. They were One Voice, all together, and it was beautiful.

Soon however, slowly and only one or two at a time, people began to add more. Someone added a note of harmony, another a descant to the melody. And even though each new note seemed just as right as all the others and only made the singing that much more beautiful, when it happened the song leader always stopped them. It was easy to spot the ones who had found their Own Voice. They were different, but she couldn't quite describe how.

She always felt a little sorry for them as they got up out of their seat and walked out through the one door in the front of the room. Oddly though, they didn't seem to feel sorry for themselves.

Then one day as they were singing one of her favorite songs with One Voice all together, she began to hear a new and different sound. At first it was inside her head, a few notes that seemed the perfect accompaniment to the notes everyone else was singing. Then they were a whisper under her breath, and before she could catch herself she was singing! Loudly! Happily! A new and yet oddly familiar melody! The One Voice that was her Own Voice!

She felt everyone's eyes on her, especially his, the gaze of the song leader. She expected to see displeasure in his face. Instead it looked as if he were smiling, and she wondered why she hadn't noticed this before. She knew there would be no arguing and no other choice to be made; but truly, she didn't want to argue and, surprisingly, there was no other choice she wanted to make. She got up out of her seat, walked to the one door at the front of the room, and slipped through it.

For the next few moments she was somewhat disoriented. She found herself in front of a room full of people. They were looking at her as if she were supposed to tell them why they were there. As she wondered what to do, she looked down and shuffled her feet, frantically hoping that someone would step up and tell her what was supposed to happen next. Then she changed. It was like she grew up all of a sudden. She sensed that everything about her was different than it had been just a moment before. Now she knew exactly why she was there, and strength and confidence replaced her confusion and uncertainty. With a comforting self-assurance that commanded their attention, she declared with joy,

We are going to sing.
We are going to sing with One Voice.
We are going to sing all together.

The same notes with One Voice.
We are going to sing beautifully with One Voice,
    all together.

She paused a moment, smiled, and then added, "And when you find the One Voice that is your Own Voice, it will be time for you to leave."

Then she began to sing.

What Shall I Write
in Your Dust?

He couldn't decide if he were experiencing a dream or reality. It was so different, so impossible, it simply had to be a dream. On the other hand it felt as real and as urgent as anything he had ever experienced.

The situation was this. He was sitting on one side of a beautiful table. Across from him was someone else, someone he only knew as the Other One. The table between them was covered in the finest white dust, and it was perfectly undisturbed. There were no marks in it of any kind so that it looked almost like a fine spread of seamless cloth. Somehow he knew that it was the Other One who had brought him to this place and made him the offer he was considering.

"It's time," announced the Other One.

"I know," responded the man. "Could you explain the choice to me again?"

"Of course," said the Other One. "I will write one thing in the dust and one thing only. I will write whatever you ask me to write, and whatever it is it will become a part of your life. You may ask for anything: any knowledge, any virtue, any gift, any hope, any dream, any grace, any possession, anything. I will write it in the dust, and it will become a part of you and your life."

"Could I be rich?" asked the man.

"Yes, if that is the one thing you want," answered the Other One.

"Happy?"

"Certainly."

"What if I wanted to be able to see into the future?" he asked.

"Even that is possible," answered the Other One.

Of course he had thought of all these things before, but the actual choice was proving to be very difficult. As he thought of each possible request, he tried to imagine the consequences as best he could. He could ask for love or happiness or money or fame or anything like that, but what if he got sick and died soon? He could ask for long life or good health, but then he might be poor, unloved, and miserable. Everything good he could think of to ask for was incomplete and flawed in some way. While each choice fulfilled one hope or dream, it left some other hope or dream unprotected and potentially unfulfilled. That was why he had been sitting there for so long.

"It's time," the Other One reminded him again.

"I know," replied the man. "I know."

"What shall I write in your dust?"

The man took a deep breath. He was ready to make his decision.

"Your Name," he declared to the Other One. "Write your Name in my dust."

Suddenly it seemed as if light and song surrounded them as the Other One moved a single finger toward the tabletop.

The Carpenter and the Unbuilder:
Home

The carpenter and the unbuilder had been traveling together for quite a while, and for a long time the carpenter had not built much of anything. Every now and again he made something to stay in, but it was only for overnight and just enough to protect himself from some particularly bad weather. While this pleased him, another thought had begun to bother him. It seemed to the carpenter that he had been traveling long enough that they should have gotten to the castle by this time.

Yet the unbuilder never seemed to mention such things. The carpenter decided to raise the issue.

"How much longer until we get to the castle?" he asked.

"I can't tell," came the reply.

"You can't tell?" He wasn't sure if he should be annoyed or afraid. "Are we lost?" he inquired.

"No."

"Well then, do you know where the castle is?"

"Yes," replied the unbuilder.

"And do you know where we are?" asked the carpenter, getting a little testy.

"Yes," the unbuilder offered again.

"Then why can't you tell me how much longer until we get there? I haven't built many houses recently. I have stayed on the road. Surely you can tell me if we are close— or at least closer?"

"I can't tell."

"You know, but you can't tell?"

"Yes, I know, but I can't tell. This is one truth, one awareness you must discover for yourself."

"Is there no help you can give me? No word of advice, comfort, or encouragement?" asked the carpenter.

"I am permitted to give you one bit of advice that might help," said the unbuilder. "Be still."

"Be still? What is that supposed to mean? Can you give me a hint?"

"No."

"Why not?" demanded the carpenter.

"Because this is one truth . . . "

"I have to discover for myself." The carpenter finished the sentence. "Fine." He was not amused.

Be still. The carpenter began to wonder what this might mean and how it might relate to his journey to the castle. At first it seemed at odds with the whole idea of the invitation and the journey. After all how can you get anywhere by being still? He kept on walking. However, within a few days, he decided to stop and attempt to stay still in one place for a while. In doing so he discovered that there was more to being still than simply stopping.

At first he had to confront the thought that he must get

moving, that he should be someplace other than where he was. Then he noticed that even when he wasn't walking, inside he was still moving. Inside he was still evaluating and judging himself and his surroundings. So the next thing he concentrated on was accepting what was in him and around him and resisting the urge to fiddle excessively with everything. It didn't help that there was a beautiful stand of trees nearby that were perfect for the kind of house he needed right then.

But as each temptation, each self-criticism, and each little bit of unsettledness arose, he concentrated on wrapping *be still* around it. This was how he greeted every thought and feeling. Soon he was able to set whatever it was aside and wait. Slowly it seemed as if one layer after another of desire for what he thought he needed was being gently peeled off to expose a more perfect layer of surrender and trust underneath. He stopped worrying about where he was and where he needed to be. He stopped worrying about how he would find his way to the castle and when he would finally get there.

At last one morning he looked up and saw something he had never seen before. In front of him on a distant hill was a great, gray stone wall. He looked to the left. The wall was there too. He continued to turn around and stare. The wall was all around him, in every direction, at the very limit of his sight. Suddenly he knew.

He knew that he was inside the courtyard of the castle. Everything he could see was inside. He hadn't seen it before because of what was inside him, not for any lack of travel. He smiled and looked for his companion, but the unbuilder was gone.

And in that moment he knew, as surely as he had ever known anything in his life, that he had come to the end of his journey as a carpenter . . . and the beginning of his journey as an unbuilder.